"Have you got the guts to Be Your Own" Boss?"

By Dale Quentin

I wonder how many books, videos; tapes et cetera, and read or listen to, to study the art of **"SELLING"**. Moreover, how many did you put into practice and what have you read? All that is required to be successful at **"SELLING"** needs is plain **"BOTTLE"**. Either you have it or you have not, let me explain how I became successful sales representative.

After leaving school my first job was with Curry's, as a wireless mechanic, a job by father a bus driver for 47 years had always wanted for me, and my father got the job for me. From the onset, literally hated the job, the manager acted like a sergeant major, and for over a week sweep floors and make tea, in the end, one morning sick to my teeth, told the manager to stick his job, and walked out. With hindsight, mistake number one we all have to start on the bottom rung of the ladder, as we all have to learn discipline, and respect in life whether we like it or not, discipline is extremely important and in particular self-discipline, as in everyday life, without it you haven't got a chance.

From this point, went from job to job until finally called up to do my two years National Service. Unfortunately still not learnt to respect my superiors, and gave those who I should have respected a rather hard time, and then wondering why was always in trouble, ended up on janker's, confined to barracks, or locked up in the guardhouse. With hindsight, discipline is necessary and all the army wanted to do was to instil discipline, regrettably rejected it from the onset, once again making myself a loser.

Even when the regiment went to Malaysia on active service, would not conform to discipline, I would always fight back, had I been cooperative, as I was advised had been a good boy possibly ended up with two or three stripes on my arm. However, in those days, could never see

1

further than the end of my nose, with the world in one corner, and me in the other.

Totally unaware of having selling skills; it all began while working for Joe Lyons as a ice cream sales representative on the retail side, and supplying to shops, theatres and cinemas. My job entailed delivering pre-ordered ice cream ice. On delivering the order, would mention to the proprietor should the weather change and his sales increase out of stock quickly, suggesting he overstocks for emergencies, and could be another week before he gets another delivery. Shop proprietor was overjoyed at my suggestion and I always carried an extra variety, immediately, stock the freezer to the brim, earning myself more commission, which was nice, but genuinely meant what I'd suggested, as often when the weather had changed, the phone in the office would not stop ringing, and Lyons customers would lose out.

My manager was extremely pleased with the amount of extra ice cream I was selling, he reported to head office what I had been doing, and within a week, it was common practice throughout the company. However, within our unit, there were five other sales representatives, but I was the one that always went home with the most money.

Purely by accident managed to get my hands on some junk jewellery very cheaply, would carry some in my pocket just in case, as we delivered to cinemas and theatres, and knew many of the usherettes. Chancing my arm showed the junk jewellery to one of the usherettes, and immediately she wanted to buy some, a little naïve, having purchased it cheap, sold it cheap.

Many of the usherettes in other cinemas soon exhausted my stock, replenishing it hit on the idea of buying some cheap presentation boxes, and nicely decorated the necklace or the brochure or earrings displayed them in the boxes. By doing this recouped 150% profit, being only 23 at the time it was quite amusing, and did it more for the devilment, achieving her sale would get a buzz.

A couple of year's late, reading through some adverts, spotted one suggesting becoming self-employed by selling polish door-to-door. Contacting the company decided to give it a go, my father was annoyed that I was giving up her full-time job to become self-employed.

Nevertheless went ahead against my father's advice, and once again became quite successful, I used a small leather suitcase to display the six cleaning products, lavender polish, three assorted colourful dusters, brass cleaner, mothballs, and scouring pads.

Knocking on doors in the rain was not good, but to make matters worse the leather suitcase became sodden, so to prevent this happening, varnished it, which happened to coincide perfectly for me, as currently there was an advert on the television stating their 10 of polish could prevent your gas cooker from getting dirty. Now the case was extremely glossy, and the first item I would show to a prospective customer was that in a polish, as it was a good seller, many would ask is that the polish we see on the television. Should not have been a naughty boy, but reply yes. My suitcase covered in rain spots customers would ask, do you use this polish on your suitcase, and you can imagine what I replied, that way they bought two tins.

How would you like to be your own boss? If your goal is to become your own boss, then this book is great for you, alternately wish to have no responsibilities and receive an average wage; that is fine. Initially when you are self-employed for the first 12 months even longer difficult to take holidays, or off sick, and a mortgage even more worrying, some people are happy living in a comfort zone of employment, on the other hand apply the techniques I used, will achieve you your goal. Finally, remember it **does not** happen overnight, as nothing in life comes easy, if it does, it is not worth having.

Chapter 1

"Making That First Big Decision"

My wake-up call happened one morning whilst working as a bus driver for the London transport driving the No 47 bus out of Bromley garage to Shoreditch. Quite an early start and the first bus on the road at 4:45 am pulling up and a bus stop at Downham Way, South London, noticed many London Dockers waiting to board the bus. Dressed in their working attire, many wore a cheese cutter; noticed most had a lunchbox, being the old red Oxo tin. Have never forgotten thinking to myself, at the age of 28 years old, if I do not take my own destiny into my own hands, end I will end up like the Dockers waiting to board my bus. Not that there's anything wrong with being a Docker, as some of us choose to work for others, mainly because we are not prepared to take on responsibilities, and if the world was full of entrepreneurs, who would do the work?

Bill, my conductor in his mid-40s often asked me to work with him on his window-cleaning round. When we were on late shifts that starred in any time after 2 PM onwards, Bill would always exchange with another conductor so he could carry on with his part-time job window cleaning, as Bill preferred the early morning shifts, so that he could clean windows after completing his work as a bus conductor. Thinking the matter over decided to take up Bills offer and agreed to work alongside him. Over the next couple of years, Bill and I did all the early shifts, as we would change with another crew so that we could go window cleaning, and the additional finances much appreciated, and met some very nice people during our window cleaning afternoons, as often customers would make us a cup of tea, and have a chat.

One afternoon on reaching Shoreditch went as normal to have a cuppa tea and Bill announced he was going to pack it all in as he had had enough of window cleaning, and had problems with his knees, offered me the chance to buy his half of the round, and instead sell fish to supplement his wages. A little shocked, but Bill, now into early 50s, and never had the best of health, told him I would weigh matters up and let him know within the next couple of days.

That evening working out the income from window cleaning discovered I could earn more cleaning windows cleaning, than driving the dam bus. The next day over a cup of tea in the canteen, told Bill I was happy to go-ahead and purchase his half of the business, and we agreed on a figure of £50, which in those days was quite a substantial amount of money.

Weighing up all the pros and cons, and having the added advantage of being mortgage free living in rented accommodation handed in my notice in to the London Transport. Although feeling a little apprehensive knowing I was finally taking the plunge into becoming self-employed, knew in my heart, that with hard work having already calculated the income, there was no need to worry, as it was all down to me whether I succeeded or failed.

This was my initial step into self-employment, and from the onset enjoyed the freedom, and nice to say when asked what you do for a living? To be able to reply, "I'm self-employed". If you elect to follow not necessarily in my footsteps, but do wish to become self-employed and run your own business, the best advice I can give you is to learn self-discipline. No good lying in bed kidding yourself you do not have to get up early because you are now your own boss. That is the quickest road to disaster, which many unfortunately make, as you get nowhere in life without hard work, and most important... "**Perseverance.**

As the weeks turned into months, found myself getting involved in additional work by carrying out "Builders Cleans" and is extremely hard work, and carry out after a day's window cleaning. First job sweeping out all the builders rubbish, and detested because of the dust, once done you were on your hands and knees scrubbing floors. Next scraping paint spots off Windows before cleaning inside and out, all the builders' rubbish left in the sink cleaned and polished. The average time taken per property just over 3 hours, and received £5 pounds, normally cleaned 2 properties each evening and arrive home totally whacked out about 10 PM, and after a hot bath, glad to hit the sack.

Having put some of my earnings to one side had saved enough money to purchase a second hand van outright, to carry my cleaning materials and ladders. From the onset normally rode my bike and would carry my ladder, on occasions, subject to the customers' agreement would leave my ladder at their premises returning the following day, to commence another day's work. Now earning three times the salary I was earning as driving a bus, had opened up a bank account, nice feeling to know there was money in the bank, and quite proud of myself, a nice feeling of security.

My customers quickly spotted me driving a my van, some lovingly joked and said; there must be a lot of money made in window cleaning, there is if you are hardworking, and stick to a strict routine, which I did day in day out. Once again, fate played a hand; one of my customers asked me if I would move some packing cases for her. I did that evening, and without asking, gave me £10, for my troubles, it was no trouble, as normally it would take me four hours to earn £10, by moving a few packing cases, allowing for fuel expenses and my time, from start to finish was only an hour, a handsome profit.

Having met a young woman, our relationship turned serious, and we finally got married, remained living in rented accommodation. However, after a few months decided to apply for a mortgage. Those days, you had to have proof of earnings supplied by an accountant. In addition, supply a reference of a person of social standing. Moreover, being self-employed, produce my tax returns, after examination informed by the lender prepared to grant us a mortgage.

We were both thrilled moving into a new property, and again felt extremely proud of myself, and why not? Earned every penny by hard work, sweat, and toil, particularly from the builders cleans.

My second-hand van started to produce another source of income from my window-cleaning customers decided to advertise in newsagents' windows for the removal of single items, sure enough, more work came in. Often asked to move quite a lot of contents, but was unable to carry out the work owing to the size of my van, after some thought decided part exchange of my van for a larger one. Finally, after a lot of searching, purchased a large box 1 ton van, and placed an advert for small and light removals, the advertising paid off and the phone rang frequently, my wife acted as my secretary.

Having previous experience of bookkeeping from my window cleaning, and not difficult, all you have to do is show your incomings and outgoings, an extremely important maintain all your receipts. If you are still reading strongly recommend you heed this advice, put aside money is that will be due for the Inland Revenue into a deposit savings account, which in turn accrue interest slightly lessening your final tax bill.

My wife had no objection whatsoever initially when we went out in travelling in the van, suggested why don't we purchase a car, which made sense, as I was in a position financially to do so, which we did, and purchased on Hire Purchase over a period of 24 months a 1963 black "Ford Zephyr". Unfortunately; we did not have a garage, and parked the car outside our property on the road. A nearby neighbour who ran his own chauffeur driven business got chatting to me suggested he could use my car for work as a taxi, asked if I would be interested, provided I got the car insured for carrying passengers, explained it was all evening and weekend work. Agreed on the spot to give it a go and it was not too expensive to get the car covered for the additional insurance. Once the insurance in place, advised my neighbour, who immediately gave me work, to pick up his clients, and drive them, either to the local railway station, or some evenings, collect his clients from home, take them to London theatre, and return later that evening to collect them around 11 PM after the show. In the first month I had earned almost £200, more than covered the hire purchase instalments, and mortgage. However, after 12 months my wife as was only to be expected, concerned I was never at home. We never went out anywhere, and even that first Christmas in our new home had been out taxiing until the early hours of Christmas morning, and again on Boxing Day, not forgetting New Year's Eve. Decided there are other things in life than money, if I was not window cleaning, doing a builders clean, as most of my time was now spent working with my van.

Chapter 2

"Expanding the Transport Business"

The window cleaning business was now becoming rapidly secondary to the transport side of my business, and no regrets, as it meant finally and end to "Builders Clean," and "Taxi work" long into the night. Returning late in the evening to collect the customers some intoxicated, and on the journey home vomit in the car. Cleaning the car a long process and rid the smells, so once again, no regrets there.

After a lot of thought and planning made my mind up to purchase a brand-new Ford 35 cwt chassis and cab, having experience of wheel arches that take up quite a bit of space, decided to design my own body made by a Freight Engineering Company to my specification minus wheel arches. However, shall never forget signing the HB agreement, as the total cost of the vehicle £1800, a little under what I paid for our first home deeply concerned about the monthly mortgage and HP repayments, nevertheless determined to be successful.

With hindsight, the inception and introduction to my cold calling success pounded constantly small industrial sites, introducing myself and leaving them my business card canvassed large High Street Furniture stores offering my services for their furniture deliveries, not forgetting advertising in the local newspapers.

Another learning curve, as the more effort you put into achieving your goal, less of a wait in reaping your hard earned rewards. Having pestered profusely the manager of "Colliers Furniture", finally he offered me a contract working three days a week Monday's Wednesday and Friday delivering their furniture. In addition, "Electrodynamics" contacted me concerning deliveries of electric alternators, and yet once again lady luck was there, as they only required my services, Tuesday and Thursday, leaving me free to carry out my contract with Colliers Furniture. Thoroughly enjoyed working for Electrodynamics as their work involved many long journeys all over the country. The manager was most obliging as some nights, for example; Monday might not finish my deliveries for Colliers after 6 PM, telephoned the manager of Electrodynamics to let him know I was going to be late. He would wait until I arrived, and personally load me up for the following day's work, which often would incur leaving home at 4 AM in the morning, and not getting back until late evening, often covering a distance of 500 miles. Never forgotten a delivery to a factory in Jedburgh, Scotland, just managed to get back in time by driving through the night to carry out a full day's work at Colliers.

The enquiries for removals were coming in, unfortunately still only able to carry out small to medium owing to the size of the vehicle. However, unless their removal was urgent, persuaded the customer to have it done either in the evening, provided it was local, or, at the weekend. Found myself working seven days a week, and earning very good money, it was at this stage noticed my colleagues and more importantly, friends started to envy me, and some clearly jealous of my achievements since my days of being a bus driver come window cleaner. Personally assure will happen to **you** provided you too when you become successful, just "*Ignore* **Them**", as they lack the guts **"You Have"**.

From inception, working with "Colliers Furniture", the manager provided a young lad named Robbie to accompany me as a porter, keeping their costs down, as from the beginning they did not want me to provide a porter, to which I had agreed. Our agreement didn't stay in force very long, as the manager explained he needed his porter back in the shop to assist in unloading the lorries delivering the new furniture that were constantly arriving at the store, ask me to provide my own porter.

I never really found out what had happened, but that morning as we starting Friday's deliveries, Robbie told me he been given the sack, immediately offered him a position as a porter, and pleased to say, Robbie accepted. On returning in the afternoon to pick up another load of furniture had a quiet word with the manager, who confirmed that it was not he who had sacked Robbie, but head office, and having a cut back on staff. To cover my rear end ask do you have any objection to me taking him on, the manager was only too pleased, knowing Robbie was no longer unemployed, and assure me there was no animosity.

Robbie proved himself an excellent worker and stayed with me as I expanded, which is mainly down to Colliers Furniture, who asked me to buy yet another van to do their deliveries from two of their other shops. The manager told me head office were extremely pleased with the courtesy shown to their customers, and accept another contracts. Once again accepted, and purchased my first of many brand-new 2500-ft.^{3} pantechnicons from Sid Abrams, Manchester. Shall never forget when it arrived late one evening to see my name on the side of the vehicle was reward in itself, felt so proud, as did Robbie. My only regret, my parents were not alive to see my achievements, as they would have been so proud of me, and would have given a fortune to see the smile on their face.

Work kept pouring in, and became well-known locally in the industry, as my removal competitors, never thought I would succeed, in fact son-in-law of the boss of one of the companies, after a fallout with his father-in-law, came to work for me as my foreman, and excellent and his job. As the years progressed, found myself purchasing more vehicles, all from

Sid Abrams, as they made first-class pantechnicons, all on TK Bedford's chassis. Over the next three years ended up with five pantechnicons, having become well established had many contracts with well-known companies. Now employed 15 staff made up of drivers and porters, plus a transport manager, who carried out estimating duties, and my personal secretary and typist. My company operated in our High Street. Mentioning my name, realised everyone knew my company, even our local newspaper printed an article.

Maybe you have reached a conclusion, only referring about **Me, Me, and Me.** If I did not, unfortunately not learn the lesson of what it takes, and beg you to remember and never forget, "**Only Get out Of Life, What You're Prepared to Put In**" and **you** will never go wrong. As an example, climbing a mountain is extremely strenuous, hard work, full of pitfalls, and slow. On reaching the summit, do not think you have conquered the world, **"As with One Slip, reach the Bottom Much Quicker than You Did on the Way up". So, Remember Those You Meet on the Way up As You Will Meet Them on The Way Down".**

No doubt at this stage you're wondering when I'm going to explain how to be successful, if you've understood this up to now, **you** are on the right track, as you must **believe that you're a winner**, as there is no recognition for coming second, as you will see reading on, which takes **Perseverance.**

Like everyone in life face, the vicissitudes and traumas as I certainly did having to go through a divorce completely ruined my world. Emotionally and financially inside out and not wish on anyone. As a result, lost all interest in life and in my business, my sole aim, merely to please my wife, unfortunately, business got the better of me, and my wife became neglected, another lesson is to balance your life, otherwise if you do not see the signs, end up as I did.

When you become successful, you become blind to everything else, and every challenge the places itself before you, you know in your heart you have to win. My own particular case became severely depressed, and even today regret my actions which was at that time to sell the business, I was looking for some form of escape, and had forgot to stay calm, and only have myself to blame.

The business sold very quickly, having had previous offers before, and been declined, a prospective buyer came along, offering the right money. Sold up, having let go of the last link, unknowingly at the time holding me together hence, my depression worsened, and lost all sense of direction. It was only when one of my drivers a year later pointed out I had become a complete recluse, and to pull myself together before it was too late, and financially never knew where, or what I had blown £19,000 on.

He further pointed out that the firm was going bust owing to the incompetence of the new owner, who had no idea whatsoever in running a removal company, hearing this, straighten me out, as I was determined not to see my firm go into liquidation, suddenly I was back in the driving seat. On contacting the new owner, he finally admitted his defeat, and asked if I wanted to buy the business back, and offered such a low figure, I could not refuse.

Immediately the contract exchanged hands, contacted the firm's that originally my firm was under contract to, after a few lunches, and meetings, managed to restore the contracts, and business once again was back to normal, the only thing that remained not normal, was myself. I no longer felt the joy and excitement that the job and once presented, and a removal colleague approached me about selling up, churning it over decided it was be the best as I had somehow lost the drive I once had, decided I needed a new challenge to get me back on my feet.

However, after consideration sold the business at a profit and after a few months drifted as a partner into the estate agents world. However, the partnership was a disaster, finally forced my partner to purchase my half of the business. As his only interest were money, women and skiving, definitely not advise anyone to form a partnership, as they seldom work, and if they do, are then you are extremely lucky.

After selling my share, decided to move away from the area, and the best thing I have ever done, having plenty of money in my pocket, there was no apparent rush to get involved in anything, better to take some time, and see what develops. Offered the chance to buy a hot dog van; thought, why not? Must say I enjoyed the new venture, but quickly realised, this was not for me. Sitting in the van one day decided to go back as an owner-driver, in those days I had been extremely happy, set about selling the hot dog van, was easy to offload, and made a profit.

Sitting in the back garden drinking a glass of cold lager decided definitely to purchase a second hand 35 cwt Ford Luton vehicle as previously back in 1969. Operating in the suburbs of London with a large population; hence **"More Chimney Pots Means- More Money".**

While waiting delivery of the van, started canvassing the local industrial areas, one of the questions many firms asked, "Do You Run a Carrier Service?" However, spotted a second-hand 500 Kawasaki motorbike up for sale, taking on board a demand for such a service, purchased the bike. Calling back on the firms who had enquired, inform them we did operate a 24/7 courier service, and added the addition to my business card. In addition, advertised in the local newspaper, and placed pre-printed business cards in newsagents' windows.

It was not long before the phone started to ring the adverts were paying off, as were my cold calling around the airport's industrial sites, soon I was off the ground again, and enjoying every moment of being self-employed and an owner-driver. Nevertheless, fate or luck, often pays apart in one's life, it is only with hindsight realise lady luck knocked on your door.

Moving a woman after unloading the other end over a cuppa tea she happened to mention I was wasting my time doing the job, despite the fact, she knew I was the boss. Her advice; you would be excellent as a pub landlord, or in the insurance industry. I told her neither was applicable. Her response, why not give it some consideration, I am the manageress of employment agency, and currently audiobooks have a vacancy for an insurance sales representative. Laughing, told her I could not see myself as an insurance man, and found working as a landlord, would not be a good idea owing to the unsociable hours. By this time finished our cup of tea, and ready to move, as she handed me my cheque for the cost of the removal, mentioned she would ring me over the weekend and give me the company's telephone number, why don't you ring them, what have you got to lose.

Taking on board her comments, she was right, what did have to lose, so on Monday rang them, the job was explained by the manager as being on a self-employed basis, no wages only commission, suggested I come to the office for an interview, never forgot his phrasing "As You Sound like My Kind of Animal".

Agreeing, pop to the office the following day and instantly took a liking to the manager who was full of charisma. He explained in detail precisely what the job entailed, and monies that could be earnt, provided you carried out the job to the letter. My only reason for hesitating being self-employed, wondering to myself, could I knuckle under, and be told what to do, but assured by the manager not to make any mistakes, as I would remain self-employed, and be **my own boss.**

Chapter 3

"Discovering Unknown Skills"

After the initial interview arriving home, hearing what you can learn, decided I would try it, but nothing more, would carry on with my removals and transport work, and work part-time as an insurance sales representative.

Having made my mind up, contacted the company informing them I wish to join, and received an application form that I duly completed and returned, and was accepted. The company sent me on their initial training course that was residential to obtain my licensed to sell their products. Listening to one of the trainer's sales patter on getting new business really annoyed me based on contacting family and friends, to try to sell them a policy, and then ask for referrals, however this practice was commonly practised within the industry, further involved a lot of late nights, for me was rather off-putting. Like an idiot not paying enough attention to what stated, or making notes on the day of the test flunked the initial training course.

Feeling ashamed and annoyed on the 2 ½ hour train journey home gave myself a dressing down, on arriving home, my manager rang to say that he had been informed I had failed the exams, but the trainer had stated in his opinion   would be a top salesman. Based on this, my manager told me he was prepared to give me a second chance, and arrange to trained personally at the branch, thankfully got my licence to sell the company's products.

Still uncertain and feeling strongly against pestering those I knew, and against my principles knowing the new job entailed working late into the evening, was really a downer for me. However, plucking up courage ventured out on my first day in the industry, not knowing where to start decided to pop in in to see the person who had sold me the second-hand 35 cwt Luton van.

 Wandering into the showroom dressed smartly in a suit and tie, he was somewhat taken aback by my appearance. Enquired if everything was okay; how's the van, et cetera, informed him I had sold the van, and now working in the insurance industry. At first he laughed, then asked; fancy a cup of coffee? Yes I replied, go and sit in my office and I will bring you a cuppa. Bringing in my coffee sat down any swivel chair leaning across the desk and we started chatting, and eventually he got round to asking about insurance, being green founded it a little difficult to answer all is questions, but managed without appearing to be an in idiot, to answer them all.

He invited me to come to his home that evening to discuss matters concerning a pension life insurance and savings with his wife. Obviously, turn up as agreed that evening and most enjoyable, ended up supplying three separate policies, finally wishing him and his wife good night, returned home about 10:30 PM. My wife who was curious to know what had happened, told her I had made three sales, she too was excited.

The following day went straight to the insurance company office greeted by my new manager, asked how did you get on, presented him with the three applications and cheques. Congratulating enquired do you know how much commission you have earnt. My answer, have not a clue. Running his fingers over his calculator, looked up smiling informed me I had just earnt £1.012 commission.

I could not believe my ears; to earn that type of money would normally take three weeks, nevertheless still rather hesitant, as it could have been a temporary success. My manager informed me if you do exactly as I tell you, I will make you a very rich man, always do what is best for your client, and as your client grows, he will take you with him, those words proved so true.

Strongly opposed to contacting friends; and acquaintances and still deeply concerned visited business centres. The first obstacle the receptionist, sitting in the front office, and virtually impossible to get past her, her instructions were not to let anyone in without an appointment, which again proved difficult, as you had to disclose the company whom you represented, and as we all know, insurance salesmen are a curse.

Again, fate played a hand, feeling rather despondent, popped in for lunch at a local pub, and got chatting to the proprietor who like me enjoyed a joke or two. The proprietor enquired did I work local, obviously hoping I would be regular visitor to his pub, never once disclosed my profession, as they would take me either to be a tax inspector, accountant, or a solicitor, felt quite amusing, and would leave them to guessing as to what I did.

To cut a long story short, to get to the drift of how you become successful in selling, is to follow this advice will elaborate in detail later. My success came by initially visiting good pubs with restaurants, getting friendly and most important the confidence of the landlord, and incidentally, this does not happen overnight and is where determination and perseverance play their part. Moreover, once the proprietor trusted you, divulged without asking who the businesspeople were who came in for lunch every day?

This made it extremely easy, as he would address them by their Christian names, and then say to me; "that's Charlie the boss of his Smiths Engineering" knowing he could be a likely candidate, on I contact smiled, to which the prospective client responded, and it wasn't long before we were chatting. During the course of the conversation, the prospective candidate would ask… "What do you do for a living, as you come in here a couple of times a week; do you work local?" would reply, "No I just come in for lunch, I like the pub, and the food is great".

This was the start of realising I didn't have to do go knocking on doors, neither reporting to the office and cold calling on the phone from Yellow Pages all **you** have to do is simply go for lunch in the pub each day, and become friendly with the pub landlord or landlady whichever is applicable. In addition, the last thing you do is to disclose your occupation, or attempt to sell a policy to the landlord/landlady, wait and abide your time, and in most cases, after they discover your profession, which will be disclosed by the customers you've now approached and sold a policy to the landlord/landlady will ask you for advice. Provided he or she have confidence in you as it is far easier to sell to a friend, than a complete stranger is.

Chapter 4

"Follow These Instructions"

Assuming you fully understand the implications, and decided to become self-employed, if you do as I did, most will succeed, provided you have the drive determination, and most important of all, perseverance, your succeed.

You can use these sales tactics right across the board in most sale fields, whether tangible, or intangible.

Look upon yourself as a very clever "Bakers Rounds Man" who has not established around, to put it crudely, without a round, unlikely to make any dome!

The first step provided you are in a position financially, is to select a good class public house in whichever area, or areas you intend to work. The larger the area, the better the rate of prospective business, if you live in an urban area, makes prospecting much easier, as less time and expense is spent travelling, but not be a barrier for anyone living in semirural areas.

Personally stuck rigidly to working five days a week would leave home around 10:30 AM pending on the day always home in time for tea,

Monday to Friday, and strongly recommend initially anyway, you do the same.

Remember, this is extremely important, you do not get **a second chance** to make a **first impression**, when you enter your first selected pub, this is where you will conduct your business operation, and if you read and follow me in what I did, will find success. First step is to politely introduce yourself to the proprietor of the pub, make complimentary comments about the décor, its situation, its parking facilities, and the layout of the bar. Should the proprietor be a female, do not pile on the charm, as it is off-putting, and embarrassing to the proprietor, as everyone likes to chance there are, do not attempt to flannel the landlady, and do not divulge your profession, cannot emphasise this enough.

Arrive around 11:30 AM, and after ordering your drink, and remember not to drink it quickly, as you are not there to enjoy yourself, you are there to make select potential clients. Do not approach the proprietor at lunchtime being and extremely busy time, and will certainly not want to talk to you, but if there is a Barman, take the initiative to find out who frequents the pub. Normally 12:30 PM, the /prospective clients will fill the pub, and an excellent time to listen as they bid good morning to one another ensure you make a note of their Christian names, more importantly, indicating they are regular visitors at lunchtime. The big question for you is; are they a boss of their own business? Moreover, what you need to find out in a most subtle way, seeking the opportunity to strike up a conversation, such as, this is a nice pub; I take it you come here often? Wait for their response, and progress from there.

Pubs with restaurants have their own special social atmosphere, so listen to other people's conversations discreetly, also a good time to make yourself known to the landlord/landlady, remember again not to disclose your profession, if pressured, personally would say, **"If I Tell You, You Won't Speak to Me Again"** and immediately aroused curiosity ask are you a tax inspector? To which you will reply; No, then you are an accountant, whatever they suggest just say politely **NO**, this in itself causes interest have been there, read the book, and worn the T-shirt, it works, and the longer you remain anonymous regarding your profession, the more they will want to find out, this way they come to you.

Strongly recommend popping into WH Smith and purchasing lined index cards come in a box with an alphabetical card index, one of the best investments to make, and one of the best investments you will ever make, as you can store all the relevant information about your prospective clients, and when out prospecting, and popping back on client you've already approached, read the update, and refer to your latest note. Example I had two teeth out, you can comment, trust your gums are healed now, another example, my daughter is taking her A-levels. You can then enquire as to did she pass, which will impress your prospective client, knowing that you remembered, and will be ensuring a feeling of confidence in you.

Assuming the time from speaking to your first prospective client, (personally speaking), roughly 5 to 6 weeks, in some cases less, which over the period of visiting the pub noted anything personal, or whatever, the prospective client let slip whilst talking to you. Obviously not while you're speaking to him or her, you memorise, and then write your notes on your card, and store their card appropriately in alphabetical order according to his surname, or which is easier for you. For example;" My daughter only seven years old has had chickenpox" or "I hurt my knee playing golf, and undergoing physiotherapy at the moment". Just to give you an idea, as when the time comes you can refer to the card and enquire as to how his daughter is or his knee, this way convinces the prospective client you've taken a personal interest, which makes the sale much easier, as we all like to be remembered, **Don't We?**

At the end of six weeks provided you have worked as advised, and no excuses for rainy days, should have at least 14 good class public houses that you frequent a couple of times a week, or which is ever preferable. According to the situation you have personally created, and should be on relatively friendly terms with your prospective clients, and over a beer or two an excellent time to say, "I just happened to be over this way again today client wanted to increase his pension contributions". By doing this, the prospective client knows that you are now in the insurance industry, and you can ascertain from his or her reactions whether you are likely to succeed in turning him or her into a client.

Your prospective client will be relieved to know finally your profession, and normally ask how long have you been in the industry? Always speak the truth as there is no shame in being a beginner in whatever profession, you use the sales script for. We all had to start somewhere, and remember you know his profession, and know he is the boss of his own company, feel intimidated because of his position. Nevertheless, when he sits on the toilet in the morning, is no different to you. (On a positive note once having become successful; drove a much better car the Manager Director... client, **Fact.**

The sales point reaches a climax brought on by the prospective client, who normally states, I'm glad I've got to know you, never had any time for insurance salesman, in my book they're all crooks, you reply, "Yes, but in any industry there are good and bad the problem is, the good are condemned along with a bad. "The prospective client normally acknowledges your comments.

At this stage of the game, normally be invited back to his company, or home, to either review is existing policies with another company, or chooses to discuss insurance in greater depth, your first step to success.

At the initial meeting do not and cannot emphasise how many sales people fail because they will go on and on with their sales pitch which they have learned by heart about their products. When the secret is to **listen** to what the prospective client requirements are, look on yourself now as a tailor, and explain to your prospective client precisely what your company can provide to suit his or her requirements.

Personally speaking again, my marketplace in which I felt comfortable working in, Directors Pensions, for the self-employed Personal Pension Plans, and Company Pension Schemes. Equally could have been selling double-glazing, motorcars, in fact anything, if you adopt this simple system, it will function in any industry.

Once you've carried out your fact find/or money they are happy to part with/and can afford on your prospective client's needs, just like a tailor, whose measured you for your first suit will make sure it fits perfectly. Do not get carried away knowing you can earn enormous commissions by selling the wrong products, simply advise the client accordingly, explaining all the dos and don'ts, and let the client decide which policy suits them the best.

Remember your prospective client has no idea of costs involved and will look for that information from you, in some cases it is quite difficult pending on the prospective clients financial status. Normally ask as to what they should pay, using diplomacy is the best way, and further will assist the prospective client in ascertaining their current financial situation as to what they can afford on a monthly basis.

As an approximation to test the waters, and remember always to go well over the minimum, as if you quote the minimum, and the prospective client either says no, or cannot afford that amount of money monthly, the sale is finished.

Simply inform the prospective client someone in his position normally pays £250 per month, and then remain silent, watch their reaction and you will know straight away whether they can afford that sort of money. They will immediately agree, which means you have won, or state; I can only afford £150 a month, and you have won again. At this point, close the sale and opening in front of your prospective client the application form, and immediately ask; do you have a middle name? At the same time, start completing the application by filling his Christian name, pause and wait for the answer to the middle name, at this stage the client will accept he is going to proceed. Once the form is completed, obtain the clients signature, or if a joint application, both signatures, now you ask for the check for £150 made payable to (......), after the sale congratulate your client on making a wise decision, and explain that you will be popping in from time to time to make sure everything is fine. At this point, it is up to you how you bid your farewell, always ensure it on a positive note.

 Remember there is always a minimum price or charge for whatever product or goods you are selling, for example, could be £50. Never ask the client what they can afford, if you do and they answer £25; your sale is dead in the water, as you cannot pump water uphill, always ask for a higher amount, that way you will succeed.

If you followed the pattern, you should have achieved at least five sales at the end of the six-week period, but the pattern is repetitively, and ongoing throughout your career as a salesperson. There is no reason why you should not succeed, in your first year right off the first six weeks, as that is the hardest part of establishing a footing, and receiving your commission. If you have read this far, I am convinced you are going to be successful as a salesperson, and to give you an insight as to your client bank. There are 52 weeks in the year, you have just spent six weeks canvassing, and your success rate is five new clients, based on this figure, allowing for two weeks holiday possibly a couple of weeks off sick, and allowing for bank holidays. Base your canvassing time to be spread over 36 week period, means on the sixth week you should have signed up another five new clients annual achievement 35 new clients.

This is a conservative figure assuming you carry out your as specified your approach searching for new business, and that once the client is established insuring as promised you call back on them. If you have assure you they will refer you to and other business associates, and again rests with you, as selling is extremely hard whatever you happen to be selling; remember; "There Is No Endurance, like a Man Who Sells Insurance". Furthermore applicable if you are sincere about selling in any line of work, and essential that you have self-discipline, as without it you will not succeed, speaking personally have worked with over 800 sales people, out of which a small minority was successful, you may ask why, because they had first of all determination and the will to succeed. On a negative note but for your own benefit if you feel that you do not have the following qualifications, please do not enter into the sales world, and if you do, most pleased to hear from you if you prove me wrong.

Chapter 4

"Qualifications Required for Success"

First of all please do not think I am some smart arse trying to pull the wool over your eyes assure you I'm not, I'm just an ordinary guy who's been successful selling and I'm going to tell you why, and if you fit the bill, you will be as successful.

All my life have loved and enjoyed socialising, being with other people, love to hear and tell jokes, and thoroughly enjoy a good laugh as most of us do, as it is good for your health anyway. Personally got on with folk from all lifestyles and if I am honest, and it always pays to be honest, enjoy being in the limelight, it is rewarding being recognised even if you happen to be an idiot, as it makes others laugh, and laughter is good for the soul.

Basically am trying to explain, until reaching the age of 48, when I entered the insurance industry, on the initial training course although I failed it, continually acted the clown merely to amuse others on the course, as well as the trainer. Nevertheless, through my naiveté, and not paying attention to the trainer, became the biggest idiot of all. After two weeks and taking my final exams to obtain my licensed to sell the company's product, completely flunked it. Will never ever never regret the dressing down I gave myself on the journey home on the train, but because of my clowning, as you read earlier, within the insurance industry anyway, was a notch on my belt for becoming a good salesperson, furthermore completely and utterly unaware of, as you could be at this moment in time.

So the qualifications required to be successful, not necessarily in the insurance industry, but in the selling world, is to enjoy other people's company, and speak to them not purely to obtain a sale. Primarily because you like them, and enjoy their company, personally discovered impossible to deal with anybody I did not like, and would often not pursue matters after a few words of exchange with the perspective client.

If you feel you have an outgoing personality, and seem to be the life and soul of the party, you would succeed in the insurance or any other industry, provided you can stand rejection, but following my route to success never encountered rejection why? Let me explain, had I followed the sales procedure issued by the company, was rather like one of those idiots you lift to listen to when you receive a cold call on the blower, instantly know they are reading their script from a clipboard. Which in itself is off-putting, and destroys the personalisation of the conversation, and humans enjoy, that is why most of us put the phone down when we receive a cold call, as it is all a load of verbal diarrhoea.

The average sales approach is as I'm sure would agree "Good Afternoon my name is CU Cumming and represent Long-Term Insurance Ltd" can I interest you in a policy, will if you take that line you will normally end up being told to piss off, as straightaway, the approaches got right up your back. As like everyone hate insurance, especially those who try to sell it, and take your vengeance out on the individual representing your biggest hate.

One-way to look at insurances, if you were getting on an aeroplane and offered a parachute, most of us would take, as it would make you feel secure in case of emergency. Moreover, arriving at your destination, a relief to return it to the airline knowing there was no need to use it. Well that is exactly what insurances is, nothing more than a parachute or for the sake of a better word a safety line. Imagine you have returned from a winter's holiday, back home in the UK, a cold front, has caused your pipes in the loft to burst, and your home is flooded out. What a relief to know that you can ring your insurance company and they will provide accommodation and if required rebuild your home. And at the end of the day only costs a couple of quid a week, the only idiot is the one that declines taking out a policy, and then when an accident happens, blames everyone else but themselves.

But enough about insurance, the sole purpose is to explain the art of selling without causing annoyance to the prospective client, cold calling today is banned, but by using this simple method, you will succeed, provided you have as explained the character, determination and willpower, ambition, and drive it impossible to fail.

Your rewards once you become successful in the sales world are phenomenal, in 1984, after six weeks working on a company pension scheme and £17,000 biggest sale ever. In fact was earning more than the Prime Minister in those days, and completely unaware as to why I was a success, as all I ever did was to go into a nice pub for lunch, and socialise, it really was that simple, all I needed to do was to get to know successful people.

My manager often used to say if I had to more in the branch like you, I could get rid of the other 23, and at the Monday morning meetings when we would discuss, Appointments, Sales, Closing Sales, Next Week's Appointments, I was first on sales and closing sales, but never had any appointments, owing to the way I operated.

My manager would use me as an example to the rest of the direct sales force within the branch, and make me stand up, do a twirl. Turning to the rest of the salesman, ask, take a good look, he's got a head, two arms and two legs, and a tongue, exactly the same as you, and all he does is goes out and speaks to people, how simple can that be?

That really says it all, because the way I elected to operate, being against the company's sales spill, suddenly found myself as the fourth top salesman out of 800 within the company, and all I ever did, was be myself. If you feel your character in any way is similar to mine, then you two are what they call in the industry a natural born salesperson, and without fail succeed.

These are the basic principles you must follow to succeed, activity, this is the only way to create a rapport with perspective clients, the more activity, and the more clients you will get, remember you are looking for yeses, and each no will bring you nearer to a yes.

Secondly, you must be persistent, persistency always pays off, but whatever you do, do not make yourself a nuisance. You will always get those that will tell you they want to think about it or make a feeble excuse purely to get rid of you, this is where persistency counts, as most people will take it that the prospective client is not interested, and never go back, that is a big mistake. All you do is thank the person for their time, comment it was a pleasure talking to them, casually just say on the way out; next time I am in the area, I will pop in to see you. Speaking from experience most of my clients admitted eventually the reason they dealt with me is because I had kept my word and kept coming back, and felt safe dealing with me. As a prospective client who is about to pay quite some considerable amount of money over their lifetime, needs to feel confidence in the person they are dealing with.

It may sound boring but it's important at the end of each day, to jot down a few notes on wave been and extremely important to make a note of those people showed promise as becoming clients, vehemently emphasise do not take rejection personally, just think how many times you said no, and then change your mind. Never let a negative fall go through your mind, as once you get into the negative bracket, you will spiral quickly downwards.

How many times have you been in a situation, where a person no matter what you say disagrees and advises you it will not work? Rapidly with that attitude take over, and if you let them will pull you down to their level, there are all **LOSERS** and why they adopt this attitude, remember if you remove the **T** from, I **CAN'T...** *It says.* **I CAN.**

Whichever line of business, always stayed touch with your client, so often once the sale is being achieved, is on with the next one, and the next one, and so on. Ask yourself one question, do I like to be remembered? Of course you do everyone does, so **always** stay in touch with your client; it will pay dividends remembering their birthday, and send them a card also at Christmas building trust between you and your client is the best investment you ever make.

If you do not rest assured someone smarter will call on your client and with charm and sales patter convince your client its far better placing his business with him. Therefore if you have filed to make contact with the client since inception, will lose him, and cancel his order or policy with you and move elsewhere, and have only **yourself** to blame.

Let us assume you have followed all the advice, you will now have a successful client bank, now become friends, remember always to thank them for their business, and their trust they have placed in you, as without them you could have never been a success so in a way they are like your employer, which is true. You are the only one that can control your destiny, and repeat never allow those people with a negative attitude towards life to pull you down. They are life's failures.my guiding principles in life have always been "failure begins where trying ends". In addition, from small acorns, mighty oaks grow, always believing yourself, set goals that are achievable, and once again remember "The **Only Real** **" Failure in Life, Is to Give up Trying".**

Thank you for reading, sincerely hope **YOU** reach the realms of success set yourself to achieved, as selling is rewarding in many ways giving job satisfaction.

Personally, despite being 35 years on still receive Christmas cards from many of my clients showing their thanks, purely because as my manager explained to me from inception, always did what was best for your client, and as they grow, you will grow with them and always did.

"Good Luck and Good Hunting"

The End